W9-BZH-981

HORIZONS

Learning to Read

Fast Track A–B
Textbook 2

Siegfried Engelmann

Owen Engelmann

Karen Lou Seitz Davis

SRA/McGraw-Hill

Columbus, Ohio

Illustration credits

Dave Blanchette, Cindy Brodie, Daniel Clifford, Susanne Demarco, Pam Faessler, Kersti Frigell, Ethel Gold, Meryl Henderson, Ann Iosa, Susan Jerde, Anne Kennedy, Loretta Lustig, Pat Schories, Jeff Severn, Charles Shaw

SRA/McGraw-Hill

*A Division of The **McGraw·Hill** Companies*

Printed in the United States of America.

Send all inquiries to:
SRA/McGraw-Hill
8787 Orion Place
Columbus, OH 43240-4027

ISBN 0-02-687510-1

5 6 7 8 9 VHJ 05 04 03

k j h w th g c

1. has
2. his
3. hike
4. hill

1. wins
2. trees
3. goats
4. waves

1. crow
2. green
3. read
4. need

1. filled
2. sailed
3. mailed
4. lived

A goat ate and ate. The goat said, "I feel sick."

A mole told the goat, "You need to sit and read."

The mole gave the goat a note. Did the goat read that note? No. The goat ate it.

I feel sick.

You ate the note.

u h n c g t u j

1. green
2. grow
3. c**oa**t
4. note
5. fit

1. had
2. hid**e**
3. hid
4. hold
5. hom**e**

1. smil**ed**   2. liv**ed**   3. s**ai**l**ed**

4. fill**ed**   5. kick**ed**

A crow had a green coat. A goat said to the crow, "I like that coat."

The crow said, "No goat can fit in this coat."

The goat said, "May I try?"

The crow gave the coat to the goat. The goat said, "This coat will fit in me." And the goat ate the coat.

I like that green coat.

This c<u>oa</u>t fits in me.

52

8

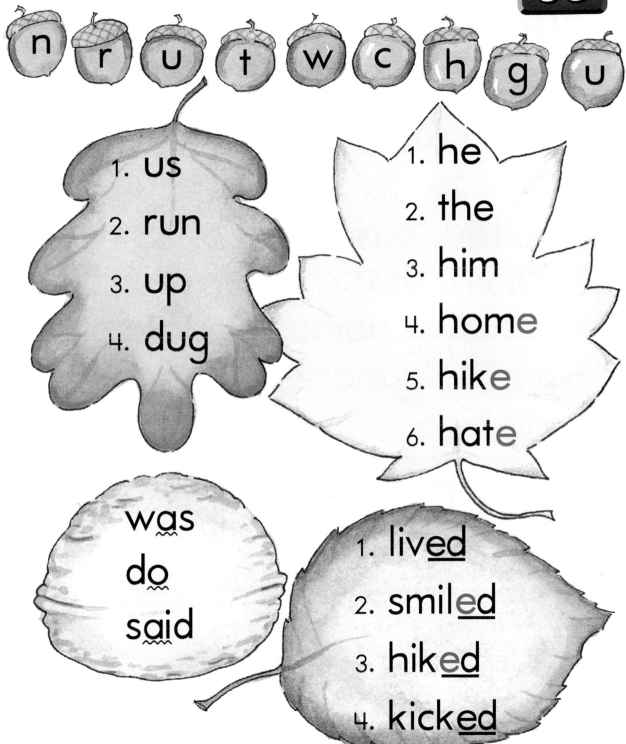

n r u t w c h g u

1. us
2. run
3. up
4. dug

1. he
2. the
3. him
4. home
5. hike
6. hate

was
do
said

1. lived
2. smiled
3. hiked
4. kicked

9

A crow told his dad, "I hate to fly, so I will hike."

The crow hiked over five miles. That crow was sad as he came home. He told his dad, "No more hikes for me."

That hike gave him sore feet.

No more hikes for me.

d u n t v k g

1. hug
2. run
3. us
4. up

1. was   2. to   3. said
4. do

1. hear
2. hope
3. greet
4. land

1. stones
2. liked
3. homes
4. miles
5. kissed

An ant said, "I need to go home." It was five miles to his home. A crow said, "I can take you home. Hold my tail and we will fly."

In no time, the crow and the ant came over an ant hill. The ant told the crow to land. And the ant gave the crow a kiss.

15

u d k n w h c g

1. sun
2. fun
3. us
4. rug
5. run

1. into
2. was
3. stones
4. pigs
5. rides
6. sees
7. caves
8. waves

1. grow
2. grass
3. hear
4. him
5. had
6. his

A seal said, "I like to ride waves."

That seal was in waves near caves. The seal will ride a wave into a cave. The wave will take the seal over stones.

Will the seal like the ride? No. The ride will make the seal sore.

h w b g c b u

1. here
2. home
3. hole
4. fine
5. leave
6. stay
7. slid
8. into

1. mud
2. dug
3. up
4. run
5. sun

some
won
from

A mole had a fine home. That home was in a hole. A toad slid into the hole. The mole said, "Leave my home."

The toad said, "No. I like it here and I will stay."

The mole said, "If you stay, I will go."

And he did.

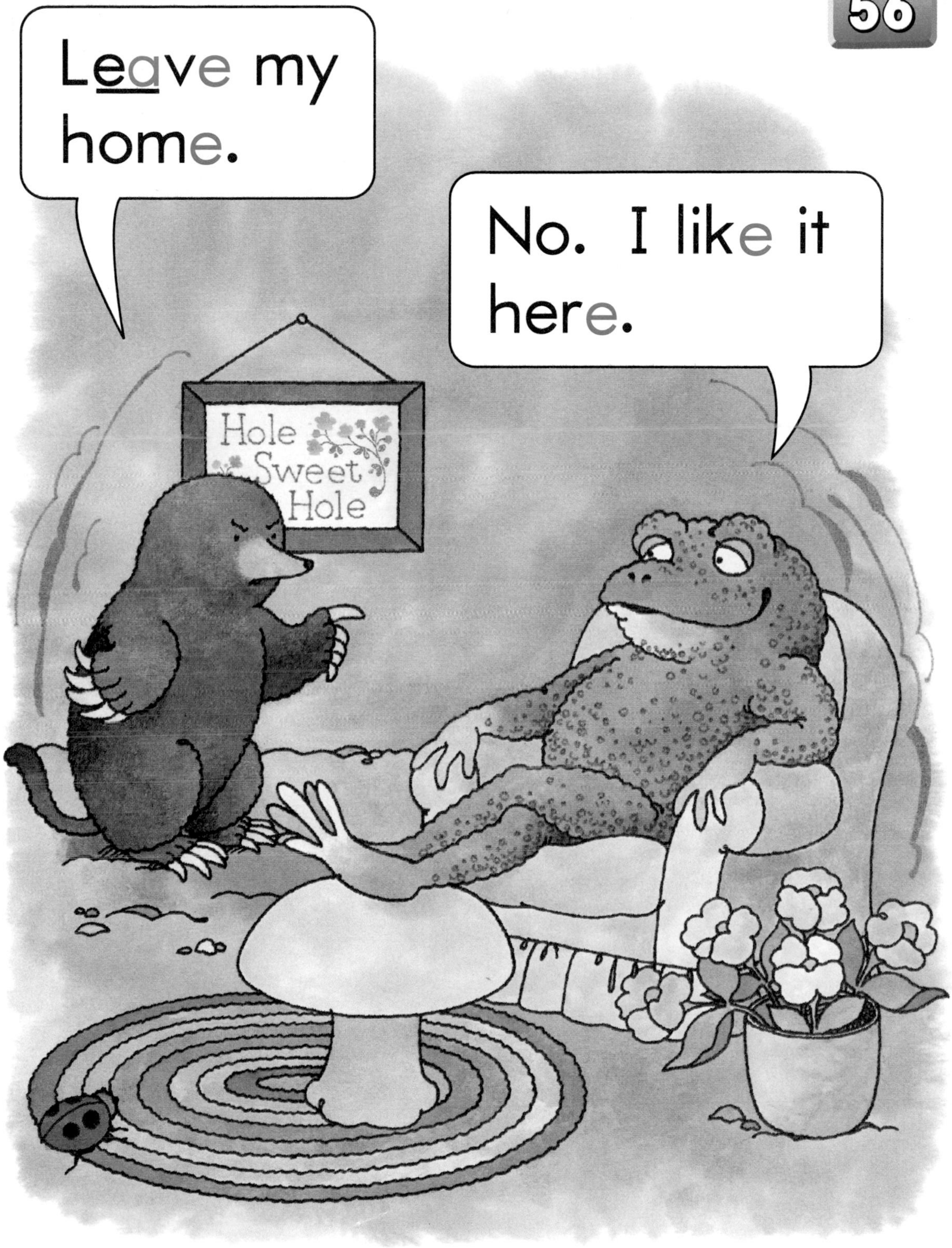
Leave my home.
No. I like it here.
Hole Sweet Hole

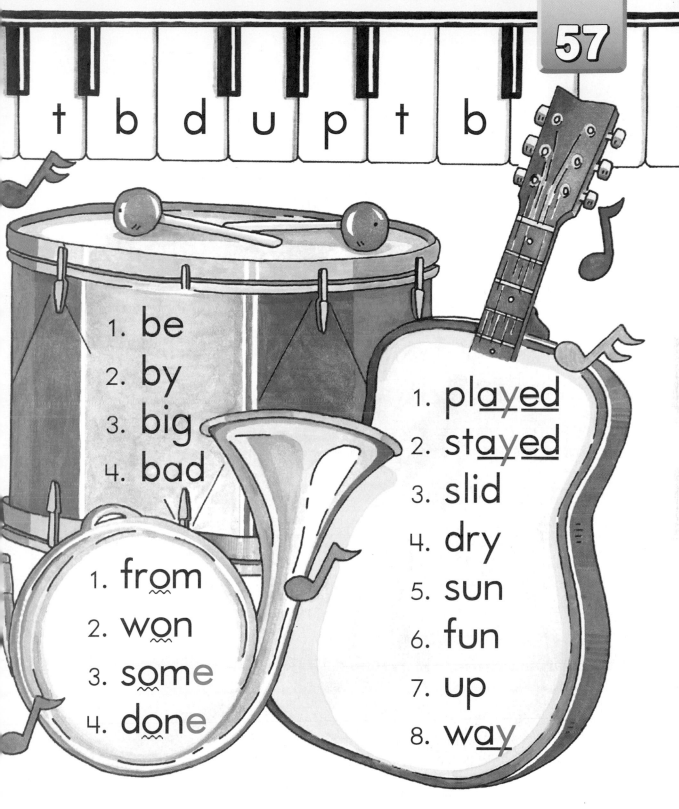

t b d u p t b

1. be
2. by
3. big
4. bad

1. played
2. stayed
3. slid
4. dry
5. sun
6. fun
7. up
8. way

1. from
2. won
3. some
4. done

Five cats had fun at a lake. 2 cats played with a mole. 2 cats ran up a hill.

1 cat slid into the lake.

Do cats like to play in a lake? No. Cats like to stay dry.

So the cat ran from the lake and sat in the sun.

Five cats had fun at a lake. 2 cats pl<u>ay</u>ed with a mole. 2 cats ran up a hill.

1 cat slid into the lake. Do cats like to play in a lake? No. Cats like to stay dry.

So the cat ran from the lake and sat in the sun.

u h b d h w b

oa

ay

1. by
2. big
3. but
4. grab
5. bug

1. said
2. was
3. some
4. do
5. from
6. to

1. hide
2. hid
3. pile
4. hay
5. green

A goat ate a green coat. So the crow was mad at the goat. The crow said, "I am cold."

The goat said, "I know a way to keep the cold from you."

The goat told the crow, "Go to that hay pile and hide in it."

So the crow hid in the hay.

I know a w<u>ay</u> to keep the cold from you. Go hide in the h<u>ay</u>.

b h u d p b g

oa
ai

1. grab
2. bug
3. dug
4. dig
5. big

1. of
2. done
3. some
4. come

1. Al
2. pal
3. named
4. tail
5. we
6. fly
7. kite
8. these

An ant named Al told his pals, "We can fly."

These pals said, "No, no, no."

Al said, "Come with me and you will see."

Al and his pals ran to a kite. Al said, "Grab the tail and we will fly."

The kite sailed over the trees. The ants said, "We can fly."

b w ai ea th h u ay

can't
didn't
don't

1. of
2. done
3. come
4. from

1. Bob
2. have
3. asked
4. three
5. last
6. but
7. mud
8. must
9. jump

The Hill of Mud
Part 1

Bob asked his dad, "Can I go for a hike with my pals?"

His dad said, "You may go, but you have to stay near the path. And you have to come home by five."

Bob and his pals hiked for three miles. At last a pal said, "I see a hill of mud."

More to come.

Can I go for a hike with my pals?

You may go, but you have to stay near the path. And you have to come home by five.

61

43

th   ck   ai   ea   oa

1. it's
2. didn't
3. don't
4. can't

b   d   v   t   p   g

1. <u>othe</u>r
2. hav<u>e</u>
3. <u>of</u>
4. <u>ea</u>rs
5. t<u>ea</u>rs
6. these
7. big

1. st<u>ayed</u>
2. pl<u>ayed</u>
3. fast
4. last
5. come
6. some

The Hill of Mud
Part 2

A pal said, "We can play in that big hill of mud."

Bob said, "But we have to stay near the path."

The pals said, "You stay. We will play."

But Bob didn't stay. He played in mud. At last some of his pals said, "It is time to go home."

Bob didn't hear his pals. Bob had mud in his ears.

More to come.

You st**ay**.
We will pl**ay**.

wh th ck ai ea oa

<u>wh</u>y
<u>wh</u>ile

1. <u>o</u>th<u>er</u>
2. hav<u>e</u>
3. d<u>o</u>n<u>e</u>
4. be
5. by

1. div<u>e</u>
2. hiv<u>e</u>
3. mor<u>e</u>
4. sor<u>e</u>
5. told
6. hold

it's
didn't
can't

The Hill of Mud
Part Three

Bob played and played. At last, some of his pals told him, "It's late. You must run to be home by five."

As Bob ran home, a man said, "I see a hill of mud that can run."

Bob made it home by five. His dad said, "But you didn't stay near the path." So Bob can't hike with his pals for a while.

The end.

It's late. You must run to be home by five.

wh th g h b d j

wheel
why
while

1. gear
2. dear
3. tear
4. hear
5. rear

1. rode
2. bee
3. Ann
4. some
5. sore
6. hive
7. games
8. bikes

Dear Dad,
    The other day we rode bikes to a lake. We ate and played games. I had my gear near a bee hive. Bees gave me some tears. I have a sore ear, but I can hear. And I have a sore rear. So I can't sit.
                    From Ann

Note to Dad

Dear Dad,
   The other day we rode
bikes to a lake. We ate and
played games.

I had my g<u>ea</u>r n<u>ea</u>r a bee hive. Bees gave me some tears.

I have a sore ear, but I can hear. And I have a sore rear. So I can't sit.

From Ann

ar
ar   b   wh   d   k   th   ar   ck   w

1. home
2. this
3. while
4. hole
5. hat
6. mean
7. toad
8. fine
9. eat
10. at
11. ate
12. rode
13. bugs
14. jump

The Bug and the Toad

A toad had a fine home. A mean bug dug a big hole into the home.

The toad said, "This is my home. Don't make holes in it."

The bug said, "I can make holes if I feel like it."

The toad said, "And I can eat bugs if I feel like it."

And the toad did that.

The end.

ar

oa

ea

ai

ar

ay

1. arm
2. farm
3. art
4. start
5. barn

to
do
who

1. wait
2. while
3. blow
4. soak
5. coat
6. jump
7. wind
8. leap
9. lick
10. hear

I Wait for My Pal

I hate to wait. I hate to sit in the rain. But I have to sit and wait while it rains.

I w<u>ai</u>t for my pal. My pal is the m<u>ai</u>l man.

The r<u>ai</u>n has made him late. That r<u>ai</u>n will s<u>oa</u>k my c<u>oa</u>t and my t<u>ai</u>l, but I will sit in the r<u>ai</u>n and w<u>ai</u>t.

At last I hear him and see him. I will jump up. It's time for us to have some fun.
The end.

ea

ai

oa ay ar wh

th

1. who
2. wind
3. three
4. cold
5. hold
6. f<u>ar</u>m
7. b<u>ar</u>n
8. l<u>ea</u>p
9. fire
10. flames
11. blow

1. <u>ear</u>
2. t<u>ear</u>
3. n<u>ear</u>
4. <u>are</u>
5. f<u>ar</u>
6. c<u>ar</u>

A Mean Wind
Part 1

A mean wind made three pals cold. So the pals made a fire near a farm. The mean wind said, "I will blow and make that fire big." The wind made flames leap way up.

The pals said, "We have to keep this fire from the barn. But the pals didn't hold the fire. And in no time, that fire was near the barn.

More to come.

A M<u>ea</u>n Wind
P<u>ar</u>t 1

A m<u>ea</u>n wind mad<u>e</u> three pals cold. So the pals mad<u>e</u> a fire n<u>ea</u>r a f<u>ar</u>m.

The m<u>ea</u>n wind s<u>ai</u>d, "I will blow and make that fire big." The wind made flames l<u>ea</u>p w<u>ay</u> up.

The pals said, "We have to keep this fire from the barn. But the pals didn't hold the fire. And in no time, that fire was near the barn.

sh sh ea ay
ar
wh sh th

1. <u>ear</u>
2. <u>ar</u>e
3. r<u>ear</u>
4. r<u>oar</u>
5. <u>ar</u>m
6. f<u>ear</u>
7. f<u>ar</u>m

1. said
2. you
3. was
4. to

1. <u>wha</u>t
2. aw<u>ay</u>
3. s<u>oa</u>k
4. lick
5. sky
6. ho ho

A Mean Wind
Part 2

A mean wind made a fire leap over to a barn. The wind made a bad joke. The wind said, "Ho, ho. It's time for a barn fire."

The pals said, "If we don't hold this fire, the barn will go up in flames."

The mean wind said, "You can't keep these flames away from the barn." And the wind made the fire jump up and lick at the barn.

More to come.

If we don't hold this fire, the b<u>a</u>rn will go up in flames.

h sh s ea th ar wh sh

1. f<u>ea</u>r
2. f<u>ar</u>
3. t<u>ea</u>r
4. t<u>ar</u>
5. <u>ea</u>r
6. <u>ar</u>e

1. d<u>o</u>ne
2. <u>o</u>ne
3. don't
4. won't

1. <u>wh</u><u>a</u>t
2. began
3. aw<u>ay</u>
4. just
5. side

1. wi<u>sh</u>
2. fi<u>sh</u>
3. <u>sh</u>e
4. <u>sh</u>ow

A Mean Wind
Part Three

The mean wind said, "I will blow
big flames up the side of that barn."
But just as the flames began to
leap up the side of the barn, rain
came from the sky.

Here is <u>wh</u>at the r<u>ai</u>n said to the m<u>ea</u>n wind, "I will keep those flames aw<u>ay</u> from the b<u>ar</u>n."

In no time, the fire was no more.

The rain told the wind, "Leave this farm or I will soak you some more."

The pals said, "We like rain."

But the mean wind said, "I hate rain."

The end.

h   w   s   sh   t   th   wh

1. <u>sh</u>e
2. <u>sh</u>ip
3. wi<u>sh</u>
4. ca<u>sh</u>

ring
sing
sting

1. to
2. too
3. tw<u>o</u>
4. <u>o</u>ne
5. won't

1. oh
2. have
3. began
4. <u>wh</u>at
5. stuck
6. free
7. still

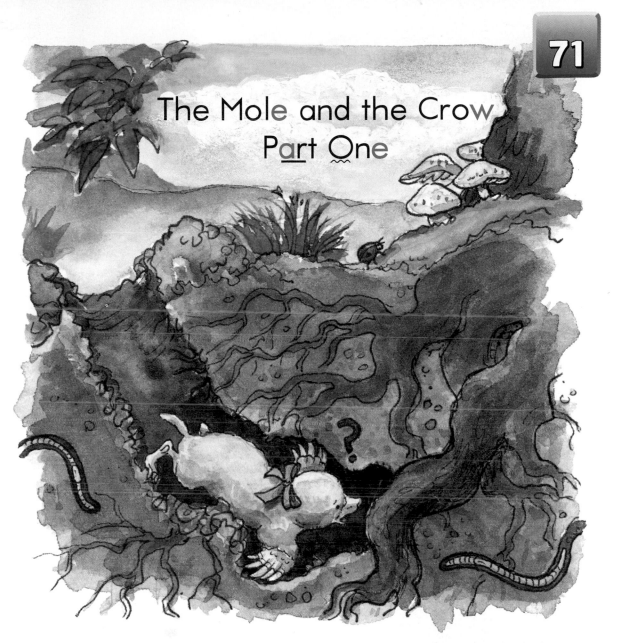

The Mole and the Crow
Part One

Moles can't see. A mole dug a
hole and ran into a tree. The mole
asked the tree, "Who are you?"
The tree was still.

A crow was in the tree. That crow said, "I will have some fun with that mole."

The crow said, "Oh, mole. You
have run into me. I am the big one.
And I am stuck in the mud. Can you
dig and free my feet?"

"I don't know," the mole said.
"But I will try."

More to come.

g b d sh th wh

72

1. this
2. these
3. <u>wh</u>ile
4. will
5. snake

<u>sh</u>ine
fi<u>sh</u>
<u>sh</u>e

1. tw<u>o</u>
2. too
3. wise
4. <u>wh</u>at
5. fr<u>o</u>m

1. sing
2. thing
3. ring
4. bring

1. h<u>er</u>
2. w<u>ere</u>
3. <u>o</u>th<u>er</u>
4. m<u>o</u>th<u>er</u>

88

The Mole and the Crow
Part Two

The crow told the mole what to do. And the mole began to dig. The mole dug and dug. At last, the mole said, "I dig, dig, dig, but these feet are big, big, big."

As the mole dug, she came to the home of a wise old snake. The snake said, "Why do you dig into the side of my home?"

The mole said, "I need to free these big feet from the mud."

"What big feet?" the snake asked. The mole told the snake.

More to come.

er   sh   th   wh
ai   ar   ay

1. <u>wh</u>at
2. from
3. of
4. thes<u>e</u>
5. fr<u>ee</u>
6. for

w<u>er</u>e
h<u>er</u>
und<u>er</u>

1. <u>ea</u>ting
2. trying
3. pl<u>ay</u>ing
4. digging

<u>sh</u>ow
<u>sh</u>ip
wi<u>sh</u>

think
thing
bring

93

The Mole and the Crow
Part Three

The mole was trying to free feet. The mole dug into the home of a wise old snake. The snake told the mole, "You think you are digging under the big one. But you are digging under a tree."

The mole said, "But the big one told me what to do."

"No," the snake said. "Some one is playing a joke."

"What can I do?" the mole asked.

The snake smiled and said, "I think I know what to do. We can play jokes, too. And I think I know a fine joke."

More to come.

The big one told me what to do.

Some one is playing a joke.

73

What can we do?

I think I know a fine joke.

97

sh th

wh ar b g

w

1. top 2. on
3. not 4. now

1. going 2. trying
3. digging 4. r<u>ai</u>ning

1. four
2. gold
3. lump
4. d<u>ar</u>k
5. oh

und<u>er</u>
w<u>er</u>e
<u>oth</u>er

need<u>ed</u>
w<u>ai</u>t<u>ed</u>
st<u>ar</u>t<u>ed</u>

The Mole and the Crow
Part Four

The wise old snake told the mole what to do. The mole came from the hole. She said to the crow, "Oh, big one, I can't free feet that are stuck in gold."

"What did you say?" the crow asked.

The mole told the crow, "Just go
into the hole I was digging, and you will
see gold."

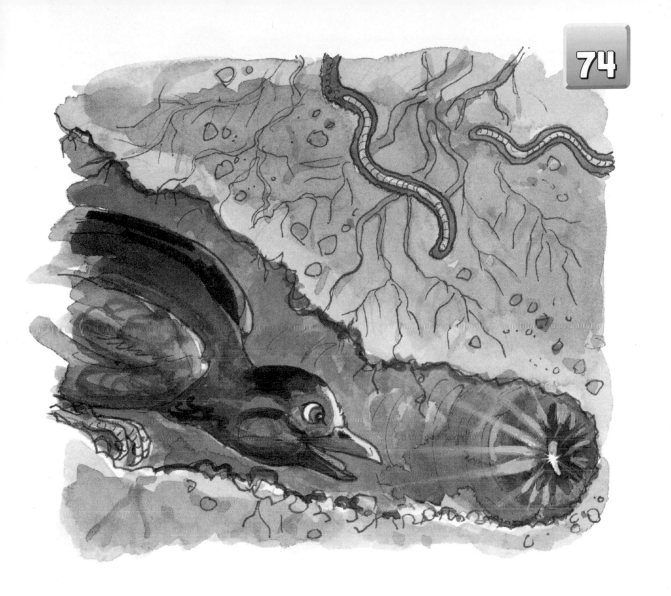

So the crow slid into the hole the mole had dug. At last the crow came to a lump of gold.

One p<u>ar</u>t to go.

i a o

1. now
2. how
3. not
4. on
5. stop

st**ar**t**ed**
d**ar**t**ed**
hat**ed**

1. spok**e**
2. <u>sh</u>am**e**
3. greet
4. becam**e**
5. pl**ay**ing
6. gr**a**b

1. that
2. teeth
3. thing
4. think

The Mole and the Crow
Part Five

"I see gold," the crow said. <u>She</u> was in the d<u>ar</u>k hole. As <u>she</u> st<u>ar</u>t<u>ed</u> to grab for the gold, it became d<u>ar</u>k. The crow didn't know it, but the gold was one of the snake's gold teeth.

The snake spoke like the big one. "Oh, bad crow," he said. "Shame on you for playing mean jokes."

The crow d<u>ar</u>t<u>ed</u> from the hole. As <u>sh</u>e st<u>ar</u>t<u>ed</u> to fly aw<u>ay</u>, <u>sh</u>e said to the mole, "You can have the gold."

That was the last joke the crow pl<u>ay</u><u>ed</u> on moles.

The end.

o er ar th sh

1. end**ed**
2. hat _d
3. hand**ed**
4. w**ai**t**ed**

1. not
2. got
3. now
4. cow
5. **sh**op

1. wins
2. **ea**ting
3. fast**er**
4. thinks
5. lat**e**r

1. wait
2. leap
3. over
4. thos
5. away

Eating Corn

A pig and a goat liked to eat. One day, the goat and pig were near a pile of corn.

The goat said, "I can eat that pile of corn."

The pig said, "Me too."

The goat got mad and said, "I can eat faster than you."

Now the pig said, "You can not."

A cow said, "Why don't you start eating and see who wins?"

So the goat and the pig started to eat the corn.

The cow said, "I think I will eat, too." And she did.

Who ate more corn? The cow.
Who ate faster? The cow.
Who got mad? The pig and the goat.

The end.

ai ea oa ar ay

i o a

Apple:
1. cop
2. hop
3. <u>sh</u>op
4. top
5. stop

Corn:
1. b<u>ur</u>n
2. st<u>ir</u>
3. f<u>ir</u>st
4. b<u>ir</u>d

Strawberry:
er
ir
ur

Pepper:
1. b<u>a</u>rking
2. h<u>ea</u>ring
3. w<u>ai</u>ting
4. l<u>ea</u>ving

Squash:
1. made
2. late
3. hate
4. time
5. while
6. wait
7. rain
8. mail
9. tail
10. soak
11. coat

Waiting for a Pal

I hate to wait. I hate to sit in the rain. But I have to sit and wait while it rains.

I wait for my pal. My pal is the mail man.

The rain has made him late. That rain will soak my coat and my tail, but I will sit in the rain and wait.

At last I hear him and see him. I will jump up. It's time for us to have some fun.

The end.

ar   sh   ir   th   er   ur

1. firm
2. hurt
3. burn
4. bird
5. shirt

a
i
o

1. lot
2. not
3. stop
4. stopped

1. with
2. wish
3. math
4. mash

1. near
2. ship
3. leap
4. barn
5. rain

1. soak
2. flame
3. more
4. time
5. side
6. here

A Mean Wind

Three pals made a fire near a farm. A mean wind made that fire leap over to the barn. The mean wind said, "I will blow big flames up the side of that barn."

But just as the flames began to leap up the side of the barn, rain came from the sky. Here is what the rain said to the mean wind, "I will keep those flames away from the barn."

In no time, the fire was no more.

The rain told the wind, "Leave this farm or I will soak you some more."

The pals said, "We like rain."

But the mean wind said, "I hate rain."

This is the end.

sh
wh ai th ea ir ur
o a i

1. hot
2. rock
3. clock
4. town
5. brown

1. Pam
2. lump
3. lamp
4. sn**ea**k
5. l**ea**ving
6. grabb**ed**
7. hiding

1. li**tt**le
2. t**ur**t**le**
3. bi**tt**er
4. bu**tt**er
5. robb**er**

118

Pam and the Gold Robber
Part One

Pam had a ship. She lived on that ship. In her ship, she had a shop. The shop was filled with lots of things.

One thing in that <u>sh</u>op was lots of
gold. Pam made gold rings and
<u>o</u>th<u>er</u> gold things from the gold.
But that gold was not in a big lump.
Pam made the gold into s<u>o</u>me thing
you see in a <u>sh</u>op. That was h<u>er</u>
w<u>ay</u> of hid<u>ing</u> the gold. <u>Sh</u>e said,
"My gold is now safe from robb<u>er</u>s."

But one d<u>ay</u> a robb<u>er</u> said, "I will sn<u>ea</u>k into that <u>sh</u>ip and take the gold from h<u>er</u> <u>sh</u>op."

This is not the end.

o   ur   u   sh   x   ir   ar

1. bitt<u>er</u>
2. batt<u>er</u>
3. butt<u>er</u>
4. aft<u>er</u>
5. robb<u>er</u>

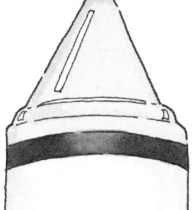

1. ow
2. how
3. brown
4. rocks
5. got
6. clocks

1. lamp
2. lump
3. grabb<u>ed</u>
4. pick
5. hidi<u>ng</u>
6. sack

Pam and the Gold Robber
Part Two

Pam had a <u>sh</u>op on h<u>er</u> <u>sh</u>ip. A robb<u>er</u> got into h<u>er</u> <u>sh</u>op to take the gold.

He said, "I see sacks and rocks and clocks. And I see a big lamp. But I see no gold."

At last, he gave up. Just as he was leaving, two cops came and grabbed him.

Later, the cops asked Pam, "Can you show us how you hide the gold?"

She said, "If you pick up the big lamp, you will know how I hide the gold."

One cop grabb<u>ed</u> the lamp. He said, "I can't pick up this lamp."

The <u>other</u> cop said, "I know <u>why</u> you can't pick it up. It's made of gold. Ho, ho, ho."

The end.

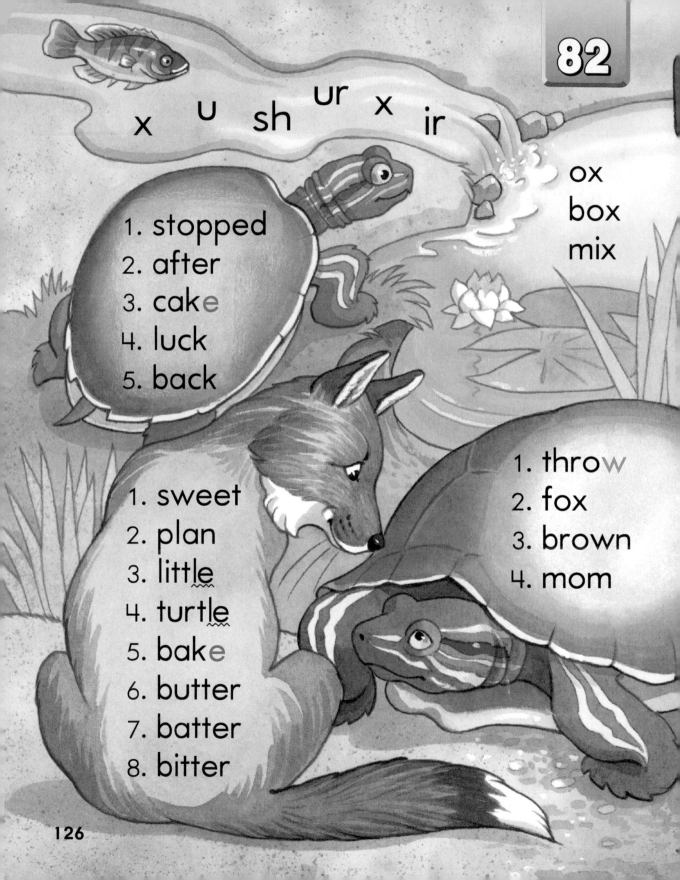

x u sh ur x ir

ox
box
mix

1. stopped
2. after
3. cake
4. luck
5. back

1. sweet
2. plan
3. little
4. turtle
5. bake
6. butter
7. batter
8. bitter

1. throw
2. fox
3. brown
4. mom

82

Bitter Butter

Part One

A little turtle asked her mom to bake a cake.
Her mom said, "We don't have butter, and we will
need butter for the batter. So go to the farm and
bring back some sweet butter."

She gave the little turtle some cash.

127

As the little turtle got near the farm, a brown fox stopped her and asked her, "What do you plan to do with that cash?"

The little turtle told the fox that she needed sweet butter. The fox said, "You are in luck. I have some sweet butter." But the butter that the fox had was not sweet butter. It was bitter butter.

After the little turtle was on her way home the
fox said, "Ho, ho. Now I do not have to throw that
bitter butter away."

This is not the end.

ch wh th sh

box   mixed   fixed

1. hurry
2. happy
3. story
4. funny

1. bake
2. later
3. showed
4. sweet
5. won't
6. done

1. tasted
2. turn
3. sold
4. turtle
5. little
6. bitter
7. batter

Bitter Butter

Part Two

The brown fox had sold some bitter butter to the little turtle. Later, the little turtle came home with that butter.

Her mom showed her how to make a cake. Her mom said, "You start with a cake batter."

131

Her mom began to make the batter. <u>Sh</u>e said, "We mix sweet butter into the batter." But the butter <u>sh</u>e had was not sweet. It was bitter. And bitter butter won't make a sweet cake.

After the batter was made, the t<u>ur</u>tles w<u>ai</u>ted <u>wh</u>ile the cake baked. At last it was d<u>o</u>ne.

The little turtle asked, "Can I taste that cake?"

"Yes," her mom said, and gave the little turtle some cake.

The little turtle tasted the cake and said, "Yuk."

More to come.

ch sh th wh

c x s k

1. wore
2. hard
3. hat
4. I'm
5. pay

1. only
2. funny
3. hurry
4. really

1. next
2. visit
3. drink
4. pond
5. taste
6. first

1. something
2. someone
3. maybe
4. return

Bitter Butter
Part Three

The little turtle tasted the cake. Did she like the taste? No. She said, "Mom, this cake is not sweet. It is bitter."

Her mom said, "How can the cake be bitter? The batter has fine things in it."

Her mom tasted the cake and said, "Yuk. That cake is bitter."

Her mom started to think. After a <u>while</u> <u>she</u> said, "Something bitter got into the cake batter. I think it was the butter. Bitter butter makes the batter bitter."

The little turtle's mom asked, "Who sold you this butter?"

"The brown fox," the little turtle said.

Her mom said, "We will go back and see him. I have something to say to him."

More next time.

sh   ch   x   c   s   k

1. <u>ch</u>air
2. <u>ea</u><u>ch</u>
3. b<u>ea</u><u>ch</u>
4. <u>ch</u>ase

1. only
2. story
3. n<u>ea</u>rly
4. di<u>r</u>ty
5. r<u>ea</u>lly
6. stormy

1. m<u>o</u>ther
2. an<u>o</u>ther
3. n<u>e</u>xt
4. visited
5. began

s<u>o</u>m<u>e</u>one
s<u>o</u>m<u>e</u>thing
m<u>ay</u>be

Bitter Butter

Part Four

The next day, the mother turtle and the little turtle visited the brown fox. The turtles had a big cake.

The mother turtle told the fox, "We have a cake
for you, but you have to <u>show</u> us that you like cake."

The fox liked things that w<u>ere</u> free, so he said,
"I like it, I like it."

"You told us you like it," the mother turtle said. "But you have to <u>sh</u>ow us that you like it."

"How can I do that?" the fox asked.

The mother turtle said, "If you <u>ea</u>t some cake really fast, we will know that you like it."

"I can do that," the fox said.

More to come.

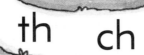

x th ch sh

1. baby
2. carry
3. <u>ea</u>sy
4. sleepy
5. body

1. shop
2. <u>ch</u>op
3. <u>ch</u>ip
4. ship
5. wi<u>sh</u>
6. whi<u>ch</u>

1. visited
2. br<u>o</u>ther
3. sister
4. summer
5. winter
6. planned

1. bik<u>e</u>
2. <u>ch</u>air
3. dov<u>e</u>
4. I'm
5. wor<u>e</u>
6. drink

Bitter Butter
Part Five

The mother turtle gave the fox some cake. He ate it so fast that he didn't taste how bitter it was. But after he was done, it started to leave a bad taste.

"Did you like that?" the mother turtle asked.

"I... I..." the fox said. "I... need something to drink."

The fox ran to the pond and dove in. He began to drink and drink, but the bad bitter taste did not go away.

"That cake is bitter," the fox said at last.

The mom said, "Do you know why?"

The fox said, "Oh, it must be the butter I sold you."

The mother turtle said, "Yes, that bitter butter made the batter bitter."

The fox said, "And that bitter batter gave me a bitter taste."

That was the last time the fox sold someone bitter butter.

The end.

x ir er ar sh ch g ol or

1. sunburn
2. only
3. hurry
4. thing
5. thank
6. spring
7. white
8. snow
9. short
10. pants
11. reach

1. Irma
2. Vern
3. summer
4. winter
5. sister
6. brother
7. hotter
8. birds
9. hard

87

145

Vern and His Burn

Part One

The winter was h<u>ar</u>d and cold. <u>I</u>rma and her brother V<u>er</u>n w<u>er</u>e w<u>ai</u>ting for spring. At last it was late spring, but things w<u>er</u>e still cold.

After five days of rain, the sun began to shine. The day turned hotter and hotter. Vern said to his sister, "It feels like summer."

Irma said, "I think I'm going to ride my bike to the lake and see the birds."

Vern planned to ride with her. Irma wore a big hat. Vern did not have a hat. He did not have a shirt. The only thing he wore was short pants.

More to come.

e o x ol or

1. your
2. you're
3. shark
4. hunt
5. ow
6. how
7. hot
8. on
9. swim
10. swam

1. thinking
2. sinking
3. closer
4. bigger

1. get
2. beach
3. shade
4. shore
5. sandy
6. really
7. sunburned

Vern and His Burn
Part Two

Irma and Vern were on the way to the lake.
The sun was hot. Irma told her brother, "You're as
white as snow. I think the sun may be too hot for
you."

"No way," Vern said.

Irma said, "But I know the sun will burn you if
you don't have your shirt on."

"Not me," Vern said. "I don't get sunburned."

I will **see** you later.

After <u>I</u>rma and her brother rode to the lake, V<u>er</u>n stopped at a sh<u>or</u>e that had a sandy b<u>ea</u>ch. He told his sister, "I think I will l<u>ay</u> on this b<u>ea</u>ch so the sun can make me r<u>ea</u>lly hot."

<u>I</u>rma said, "I am going to the <u>o</u>ther side of the lake and see the b<u>ir</u>ds. I hope you st<u>ay</u> in the shade."

"I will see you later," V<u>er</u>n said.

More to come.

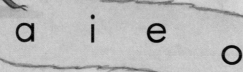

a   i   e   o

1. when
2. then
3. where
4. there

1. one
2. once
3. listen
4. because
5. does
6. doesn't
7. wasn't
8. arms
9. hurt

1. any
2. many
3. red
4. next
5. pink
6. turn
7. returned
8. became

Vern and His Burn
Part Three

As Irma was over on the far side of the lake, the sun got hotter and hotter. Vern did not turn over. He just stayed in the sand. At first, he became a little pink. After a while, he started to get really pink.

At last his sister returned. She asked him, "How do you feel, Vern?"

"I feel fine," he told her. "That sun is not too hot for me."

Later that day, Vern said other things like, "Ow, that hurts. Ow, my back hurts."

By the time Vern and Irma were home, Vern was not pink any more. He was red.

Vern's mom said, "You have a bad sunburn. Why didn't you take a shirt and a hat with you?"

Vern said, "I didn't think, but I will think next time."

The end.

1. there
2. they
3. well
4. best
5. yes

1. believe
2. Gorman
3. listen
4. because
5. wasn't
6. jumper
7. any
8. became
9. returned
10. once

1. sail
2. goat
3. play
4. pail
5. say
6. toad
7. may

The Goat and the Pail

A goat named Gorman did not see well. He liked to play with his pals, but his pals did not like to play with him. They said, "It is no fun to play with a goat that runs into you time after time."

One day, the pals were playing with a pail. One pal was a toad who liked to hop over the pail. The fox liked to jump over the pail, too. The pig didn't jump over the pail. She ate the corn that was in the pail.

Gorman told the other pals, "I can jump over that pail."

The pals did not believe him. One pal said, "You say you can jump over it, but you will just run into it."

"No," Gorman said, "I may be the best pail jumper there is." So Gorman jumped.

Did he run into the pail? No.

Did he jump over the pail? No.

What did he do? You will see.

e i y

sh
ch
or
ir
ol

1. then
2. get
3. wet
4. went
5. tell
6. yell
7. where

1. moment
2. who
3. listen
4. because
5. once
6. doesn't
7. many
8. shark

1. feed
2. clam
3. follow
4. chased
5. otter
6. Tom
7. beneath
8. bit

Don't swim near the caves.

Tom and the Shark
Part One

There once was an otter and his name was Tom.
But Tom didn't listen to his dad or mom.

One day his mom told him, "Don't swim near the caves.
Because there's a shark who hunts in those waves."

But Tom st<u>ar</u>ted playing and he wasn't r<u>ea</u>lly thinking.
He first chas<u>e</u>d a clam that seemed to be sinking.

Then he follow<u>e</u>d two s<u>ea</u>ls that w<u>er</u>e clos<u>e</u> to the shore.
He follow<u>e</u>d thos<u>e</u> s<u>ea</u>ls for a mil<u>e</u> or more.

At last he stopped to see where he was.
He said, "I saw something swimming the way a shark does."

"Oh, oh," he said, as he hid near a weed.
"I hope this is not where sharks like to feed."

e   o

or   ir   ol   ur

1. clam
2. otter
3. beneath
4. I've
5. fed
6. chased

1. saw
2. someone
3. hear
4. doesn't
5. wasn't
6. once
7. seemed
8. swam
9. snail
10. front

1. there
2. send
3. bend
4. where
5. very
6. darted
7. shock
8. shot

Tom and the Shark
Part One

There once was an otter and his name was Tom.
But Tom didn't listen to his dad or mom.

One day his mom told him, "Don't swim near the caves.
Because there's a shark who hunts in those waves."

But Tom started playing and he wasn't really thinking.
He first chased a clam that seemed to be sinking.

Then he followed two seals that were close to the shore.
He followed those seals for a mile or more.

At last he stopped to see where he was.
He said, "I saw something swimming the way a shark does."

"Oh, oh," he said, as he hid near a weed.
"I hope this is not where sharks like to feed."

Tom and the Shark
Part Two

You're as slow as a snail.

But the shark came closer and showed many teeth.
And just at that moment someone yelled from
beneath.

"For a bigger meal, you can come after me."
The otter who spoke was Tom's mom, you see.

She swam and she dove and bit the shark's tail.
She told that shark, "You're as slow as a snail."

The sh<u>a</u>rk chas<u>e</u>d Tom's mom as fast as a shot.
And said, "I've got you now." But Tom's mom said,
"Not."

Just then Tom got a very bad shock.
His mom just stopped, in fr<u>o</u>nt of a rock.

ol   or   ar   ch   sh

1. very
2. spell
3. felt
4. where
5. self
6. himself
7. herself

1. I'll
2. I've
3. man's
4. shark's
5. mom's

1. shot

2. shock

3. snail

4. such

1. front
2. which
3. chased
4. closer
5. darted
6. blow
7. hit

The shark chased Tom's mom as fast as a shot.
And said, "I've got you now." But Tom's mom said,
"Not."

Just then Tom got a very bad shock.
His mom just stopped, in front of a rock.

As the shark came closer, did she stay where she
was?
No, she darted to one side, the way an otter does.

The shark hit the rock with such a h<u>ar</u>d blow,
That he said to himself, "W<u>ho</u> am I? I do not know."

Then he asked Tom's mom, "Can you tell me wh<u>o</u> I am?"
She said, "You're a very big seal, and your name is Sam."

So Tom has a pal wh<u>o</u> thinks he's a seal.
And Sam doesn't know that Tom is a meal.

The end.

al or ar ol al ai

1. well
2. when
3. went
4. where
5. then
6. there

1. saw
2. front
3. Jill
4. six
5. fix
6. cart
7. bags
8. drove
9. town
10. with

1. driv<u>ing</u>
2. load<u>ed</u>
3. tract<u>or</u>
4. trail<u>er</u>
5. wait<u>ed</u>

Jill Went to Town

Jill lived on a f<u>ar</u>m that was six miles from town.
Jill told her dad, "It is time to go to the store."

"Well," her dad said, "I need to fix the c<u>ar</u>. So I can't drive you there now."

Jill said, "I have a plan. I can hike to the store.
Later, you can pick me up."

So Jill hiked to the store. When she got there, she got a c<u>ar</u>t and filled it. Then she waited for her dad in front of the store. He didn't show up. Then she began to think of things that may have made her dad late.

At last she saw him. Was he dri<u>ving</u> the c<u>ar</u>?
No. He was dri<u>ving</u> a tract<u>or</u> with a trailer.

Jill loaded her bags into the trailer and her dad
drove her home.

The end.

y e i o u

al ai ar al ol or

1. very
2. bell
3. fed
4. send

1. all
2. tall
3. small
4. also
5. always
6. almost

1. field
2. row
3. steer
4. plant
5. woke
6. farmer
7. digging
8. sleeping

The Farmer and the Steer
Part One

There was a steer who lived on part of a farm.
One day, the farmer drove his tractor to that part of
the farm. The steer was sleeping in the field, and
the farmer did not see the steer.

"I will dig rows," the farmer said. "Then I can
plant corn in this field."

The tractor dug up one row, two rows, and three rows. When the tractor started to dig the next row, the steer woke up.

The steer said, "What is going on? I see a farmer and a tractor in my field. I don't like tractors or farmers here."

The steer got up and said, "I will send that farmer back to his home."

How will the steer try to stop the farmer?

You will see in the next part of the story.

e o al
ol
ar

97

1. f<u>a</u>lse
2. c<u>a</u>ll
3. t<u>a</u>ll
4. <u>al</u>most
5. <u>al</u>so
6. <u>al</u>ways

1. <u>something</u>
2. <u>fl</u>ying
3. <u>landed</u>
4. <u>ringing</u>
5. <u>getting</u>
6. <u>thinking</u>
7. <u>leaving</u>

1. <u>all</u>
2. f<u>all</u>
3. bang
4. bag
5. steer
6. stars
7. set
8. bells

180

The Farmer and the Steer

Part Two

The farmer was in a field with his tractor. He was digging rows to plant corn in this field. But a steer lived here. And that steer was getting set to stop the farmer. The steer went <u>all</u> the way to one side of the field.

Then the steer ran at the tractor just as fast as a steer can run. The steer was thinking, "I will hit that tractor so hard that it will f<u>a</u>ll over. That farmer will go flying. Then he will leave."

The steer ran into the side of the tractor. There was a big bang. And something went flying. Was it the farmer or the tractor? No. The steer went flying. That steer landed on its back and said, "I hear bells ringing and I see stars."

The end.

oo   ar   al   ol   or

1. Pam
2. bother
3. pen
4. let
5. set
6. them
7. ever
8. never
9. down
10. much

1. pepper
2. everything
3. okay
4. their
5. smelled
6. called
7. six
8. dirt
9. pot

Peppers for Pam's Pigs
Part One

Pam had six pigs. Their names were Pig One, Pig Two, Pig Three, Pig Four, Pig Five and Pig Six. Pig Six was very small. The other pigs were three times as big as she was.

One day, Pam was going to feed her pigs. She didn't have pig feed for them. All she had were red hot peppers. Pam had piles of these peppers. She had never fed her pigs peppers, but she said, "I think I can feed my pigs hot peppers. Those pigs eat everything."

So she loaded some peppers in a pot and some peppers in a pan. She went to the pig pen with the pot and pan of peppers. She set the peppers in a pile and called the pigs. "Here Pig One. Here Pig Two…"

And then the pigs came. The pigs smelled the peppers but didn't start eating. Pam said, "I don't have any pig feed for you. Why don't you try eating these peppers?"

So the pigs smelled the peppers and started to eat.

More next time.

oo ol or al ar

1. soon
2. food
3. tooth
4. room

1. seconds
2. _everything_
3. pigs
4. peppers
5. piles

6. bother
7. never
8. ever
9. dirt

1. getting
2. rolling
3. saying
4. doing

1. drink
2. drank
3. think
4. thank

Peppers for Pam's Pigs

Part Two

The pigs were eating Pam's red hot peppers. <u>All</u> at once Pig Three stopped eating and started to turn red. Then Pig Five turned red. S<u>oo</u>n, <u>a</u>lmost <u>a</u>ll the pigs were red. The red pigs ran to the drinking pan in the pen and began to drink. The pigs drank and drank. Then those pigs ran here and there, eating dirt to get rid of the hot taste.

Burp.

The only pig that didn't turn red was Pig Six. She ate <u>a</u>ll the peppers from the pot and <u>a</u>ll the peppers from the pan. When she was done, she was pink, not red. She smil<u>e</u>d at Pam and said, "B<u>ur</u>p." That was her way of saying thank you.

190

Now, Pam does not feed peppers to <u>all</u> the pigs.
She feeds peppers to Pig Six. And when Pig Six eats
the last pepper, she <u>a</u>lways tells Pam, "Thank you."
The end.